THE REMINDERS

ESSENTIAL WISDOM
FROM THE HOLY QUR'AN

Copyright © 2008 by Tughra Books

11 10 09 08   1 2 3 4

Art Director
Engin Çiftçi

Designed by
Sinan Özdemir

Published by Tughra Books
26 Worlds Fair Dr. Unit C
Somerset, New Jersey, 08873, USA
www.tughrabooks.com

ISBN 978-1-59784-143-6

Printed by
Çağlayan A.Ş., Izmir - Turkey

COVER: The calligraphic letter "و" (waw), which is shown on the cover, is equivalent to the letter "w"
in the Roman alphabet. In Islamic art, this calligraphic letter is considered to stand for Wahdaniya, or
the Oneness of God. It also signifies two Divine Names: Wahid, or "The One"; as well as Wadud, or
"The All-Loving," Who is the only One to be adored and worshipped. Calligraphers thus sometimes
write this letter in the shape of a believer in prostration adoring the Wadud, the True Beloved, for no
other reason than for the love for the Creator.

The Arabic calligraphy on the spine, which is worked into a symmetrical pattern with its mirror image,
is from a Qur'anic verse which reads, *Every one acts according to his own character* (Isra 17:84).

DOES MAN THINK THAT HE WILL BE LEFT UNATTENDED,
WITHOUT PURPOSE? *

THIS IS THE WORD THAT DISTINGUISHES GOOD FROM EVIL.
IT IS NOT A THING FOR AMUSEMENT. **

THE MUTUAL RIVALRY FOR PILING UP THE GOOD THINGS OF THIS WORLD
DIVERTS YOU FROM THE MORE SERIOUS THINGS— UNTIL YOU VISIT THE GRAVES.
BUT YOU WILL SOON KNOW THE REALITY. AGAIN, YOU WILL
SOON KNOW! WERE YOU TO KNOW WITH CERTAINTY OF MIND,
YOU WOULD BEWARE! ***

---

*   (75: 36)
**   (86: 114)
***   (102: 1-5)

Foreword

The Message from our Creator is easy enough to remember,
But we are only human, after all, and we forget.
Mankind has, in fact, been remembering and forgetting, in tragic cycles,
In every niche of our expansive Earth, for uncountable millennia.

Thankfully, our Creator is All-Aware of our weaknesses,
And thus knows that we will need periodic reminders, now and again,
Of the tremendous promise which frames our existence,
Of the purpose of our journey in this corporeal dimension,
And of the critical path by which we can secure our souls.
That's why the Creator has sent us so many Messengers,
Upon them all be peace and blessings,
Since the primordial sparks of time,
Wherein were engendered the elemental origins of beings.

It is from the Last Message, the Final Revelation,
Known simply as the Holy Qur'an,
As related through the diligent and most honorable efforts
Of the very Last Prophet,
Known simply as Prophet Muhammad,
Upon him be peace and blessings,
That the essential wisdom presented here is gathered and returned
To the hands of those who simply will to hold
The "Hand" of God.

Unmatched, inimitable, inexplicable, incalculable:
From the Source of Everything comes this ultimate beckoning,
In a Voice which transcends all, and surrounds all, addressing us
At once as "I," as "He," as "Your Lord," as "God,"
Words which penetrate every point of perspective,

Articulating the varicolored views which revolve on the Axis of all that is seen and unseen,
Evoking tranquility and alertness—piercing, revealing and enticing to infinite depths,
Like a divine prism casting the most brilliant illumination
Before and behind us, beside and beyond us,
Until the full breadth of its mercy compels the most resonant harmonies in our hearts.

Seekers of truth are encouraged to reflect on the passages within these pages,
And to share them with others whom they may encounter
Along the humble course of men and women of clay,
In order to uncover the quintessential verity of the Oneness of God,
To find everlasting hope in the life of the inner self,
And to solicit shelter in this most beautiful scripture, the Holy Qur'an,
Like coming home again after the unbearable trial of distance
From a Presence so powerful and so encompassing that It dwells above the plane of names:
An Enveloping Benevolence which summons us all from beyond both space and time.

For our own awareness of the Creator's never-ending grace upon humanity
Rests in our crucial conviction that One Creator, God,
Whom we seek and entreat in so many languages,
Is not just the Pulse by which faith flows to us, through us, and from us,
And not just the Weaver of the threads by which we are bound so wondrously to one another,
But also the Genesis and the Attainment of the sojourn of each solitary spirit,
For God is the Light of Eternity.

Acknowledgment

We are grateful to Kathleen St.Onge for her inspiring contributions in the compilation and editing of this book and for writing the Foreword.

Part

Essential Reminders
from the First Person
Point-of-View

KEEP YOUR PROMISE TO ME,
AND I WILL KEEP MINE TO YOU. *

REMEMBER ME—I WILL REMEMBER YOU.
BE GRATEFUL TO ME, AND DO NOT REJECT FAITH. **

---

*   (2: 40)
**   (2: 152)

I am indeed close to them.
I listen to the prayer,
Of every suppliant calling on Me.
Let them also, with a will,
Listen to My call and believe in Me,
That they may walk in the right way. *

---

* (2: 186)

We detail Our signs
for people who understand. *

Keep your soul content
With those who call on their Lord
In the morning and evening,
Seeking His Presence.
And let not your eyes pass beyond them,
Seeking the pomp and glitter of this life;
Nor obey any whose heart
We have permitted to neglect
The remembrance of Us—
One who follows his own desires,
Whose case has gone
Beyond all bounds. **

---

*   (6: 98)
** (18:28)

Not in play or amusement
Did We create the heavens
And the earth,
And all that is between! *

We created not the heavens
And the earth
And all between them
But for just ends,
And for a term appointed. **

---

*   (21: 16)
**   (46: 3)

O mankind!
We created you
From a single pair of a male and a female,
And made you into nations and tribes
So that you might know each other—
Not so that you might despise each other!
Verily, the most honored of you
In the sight of God
Is the one who is the most righteous of you.
And God has full knowledge,
And is well acquainted
With all things. *

---

*   (49: 13)

NOW AWAIT IN PATIENCE
THE COMMAND OF YOUR LORD,
FOR VERILY YOU ARE IN OUR EYES. *

VERILY, WE HAVE CREATED MAN
INTO TOIL AND STRUGGLE.
THINKS HE,
THAT NONE HAS POWER OVER HIM? **

---

*   (52: 48)
**   (90: 4–5)

V ERILY, WE TAKE IT UPON
OURSELVES TO GUIDE—
AND VERILY,
TO US BELONG THE END
AND THE BEGINNING. *

* (92: 12–13)

Part

Essential Reminders from the Second or Third Person Point-of-View

O people! Adore your Guardian-Lord,
Who created you and those who came before you
That you may hope to attain righteousness.
Who has made the earth your couch;
And the heavens your canopy;
And sent down rain from the heavens;
And brought forth fruits for your sustenance.
Then do not set up rivals to God
When you know the truth. ✳

✳   (2: 21—22)

To God belong
the East and the West:
Wherever you turn,
There is the presence of God.
For God is All-Pervading,
All-Knowing. *

_____

*   (2: 115)

To Him is due
The primal origin
Of the heavens
And the earth.
When He decrees a matter,
He says to it: "Be!"
And it is. *

* (2: 117)

Be sure We shall test you with something of
    fear and hunger,
Some loss in goods or lives, or of the fruits of
    your toil—
But give glad tidings to those who patiently
    persevere,
Those who say, when afflicted with calamity:
"To God We belong, and to Him is our return."
They are those on whom descend blessings
    from God, and mercy,
And they are the ones who receive guidance. *

---

*   (2: 155–157)

YOUR GOD IS ONE GOD. THERE IS NO DEITY BUT HIM,
THE ALL-MERCIFUL, THE ALL-COMPASSIONATE. *

* (2: 163)

Behold!
In the creation
Of the heavens and the earth;
In the alternation
Of the night and the day;
In the sailing of the ships
Through the ocean for the profit of mankind;
In the rain which God sends
Down from the skies,
And the life which He thus gives
To an earth that is dead;
In the beasts of all kinds
That He scatters through the earth;
In the change of the winds,
And the clouds which they trail like slaves,
Between the sky and the earth—
Here, indeed, are signs
For a people who are wise. *

---

*   (2: 164)

G od loves.
Those who do good. *

G od.
There is no god but He,
The Living, the Self-subsisting,
The Eternal.
No slumber can seize Him, nor sleep.
His are all things in the heavens,
And on the earth. **

---

*   (2: 195)

**   (2: 255)

Let there be no compulsion in religion,
For truth stands out clearly from error.
Whoever rejects false deities
And believes in God
Has grasped the most trustworthy hand-hold,
One that never breaks.
And God hears and knows all things. *

---

* (2: 256)

On no soul does God place a burden
Greater than it can bear.
It gets every good that it earns,
And it suffers every ill that it earns. *

There is no god but Him.
That is the witness of God,
His angels,
And those endued with knowledge,
Standing firmly, in justice.
There is no god but Him,
The Exalted in Power,
The All-Wise. **

_____

*   (2: 286)
**   (3: 18)

BE QUICK IN THE RACE FOR FORGIVENESS
FROM YOUR LORD,
AND FOR A GARDEN WHOSE WIDTH
IS THAT OF THE WHOLE OF THE HEAVENS
AND OF THE EARTH,
PREPARED FOR THE RIGHTEOUS. *

* (3: 133)

EVERY soul shall have a taste of death,
And only on the Day of Judgment
Will you be paid Your full recompense.
Only the one who is saved
Far from the Fire,
And admitted to the Garden,
Will have attained
The object of life,
For the life of this world
Is but goods and chattels of deception. *

---

*   (3: 185)

O mankind!
Reverence your Guardian-Lord,
Who created you from a single soul,
And created from it, of like nature, its mate,
And from them twain scattered like seeds
Countless men and women.
Reverence God,
Through whom you demand your mutual rights,
And reverence the wombs that bore you,
For God ever watches over you. *

---

* (4: 1)

God,
There is no god but Him.
Surely, He will gather you together
Against the Day of Judgment,
About which there is no doubt.
And whose word can be truer
Than God's? *

---

*   (4: 87)

GUARD YOUR OWN SOULS.
IF YOU FOLLOW GUIDANCE,
NO HURT CAN COME TO YOU
FROM THOSE WHO STRAY.
THE GOAL OF YOU ALL IS TO GOD—
IT IS HE WHO WILL SHOW YOU
THE TRUTH
OF ALL THAT YOU DO. *

---

* (5: 105)

HE IS GOD
IN THE HEAVENS AND ON THE EARTH.
HE KNOWS WHAT YOU HIDE,
AND WHAT YOU REVEAL.
AND HE KNOWS THE RECOMPENSE
WHICH YOU EARN BY YOUR DEEDS. *

* (6: 3)

With Him are the keys of the unseen—
The treasures that none knows
But He.
He knows whatever there is on the earth
And in the sea.
Not a leaf falls
But with His knowledge;
And there is not a grain in the darkness
Nor in the depths of the earth,
Nor anything fresh or dry—green or withered—
But it is inscribed in a record
Which is clear
To those who can read. *

It is He Who has produced you
From a single person.
Here is a place of sojourn,
And a place of departure. **

*   (6: 59)
**   (6: 98)

No vision can grasp Him,
Yet His grasp is over all vision.
He is above all comprehension,
Yet He is acquainted with all things. *

The word of your Lord
Finds its fulfilment In truth and in justice—
None can change His words,
For He is the One Who hears and knows all. **

---

*   (6: 103)
**   (6: 115)

To God belong
The All-Beautiful Names,
So call on Him by them. *

Do they see nothing
In the government
Of the heavens and the earth,
And all that God has created?
Do they not see
That it may well be,
That their term is soon drawing to an end?
In what Message after this
Will they then believe? **

---

*   (7: 180)
**   (7: 185)

O reader,
Bring your Lord to remembrance
In your very soul,
With humility and in reverence,
Without loudness in words,
In the mornings and evenings. *

* (7: 205)

GOD HAS PROMISED BELIEVERS—
MEN AND WOMEN
GARDENS UNDER WHICH RIVERS FLOW,
TO DWELL THEREIN,
AND BEAUTIFUL MANSIONS,
IN GARDENS OF EVERLASTING BLISS.
BUT THE GREATEST BLISS OF ALL
IS THE GOOD PLEASURE OF GOD—
THAT IS THE SUPREME FELICITY. *

---

*   (9: 72)

To God belongs the dominion
Of the heavens and the earth.
He gives life and He takes it.
Except for Him,
You have no protector or helper. *

There is no moving creature on earth
But its sustenance depends on God.
He knows the time and place
Of its definite abode,
And its temporary deposit—
All is in a clear record. *

——————————————

*   (11: 06)

TO GOD BELONG
ALL OF THE UNSEEN SECRETS
OF THE HEAVENS AND THE EARTH,
AND TO HIM GOES BACK
EVERY AFFAIR FOR DECISION.
SO WORSHIP HIM,
AND PUT YOUR TRUST IN HIM.
YOUR LORD IS BY NO MEANS
UNAWARE OR UNMINDFUL
OF WHAT YOU DO.*

* (11: 123)

WHAT YOU WORSHIP
APART FROM HIM
IS NOTHING BUT NAMES
WHICH YOU HAVE NAMED,
YOU AND YOUR FATHERS,
FOR WHICH GOD HAS SENT DOWN NO AUTHORITY.
THE COMMAND IS FOR NONE BUT GOD.
HE HAS COMMANDED THAT YOU WORSHIP
NONE BUT HIM—
THAT IS THE RIGHT RELIGION,
BUT MOST MEN UNDERSTAND NOT. *

---

* (12: 40)

There is,
In the stories of the prophets,
Instruction for people
Endued with understanding.
It is not a tale invented,
But a confirmation
Of what went before it—
A detailed exposition of all things,
And a guide and a mercy
To any who believe. *

---

*   (12: 111)

HE GUIDES TO HIMSELF
THOSE WHO TURN TO HIM
IN PENITENCE—
THOSE WHO BELIEVE,
AND WHOSE HEARTS FIND SATISFACTION
IN THE REMEMBRANCE OF GOD.
FOR WITHOUT DOUBT,
IN THE REMEMBRANCE OF GOD,
HEARTS DO FIND SATISFACTION. *

---

* (13: 27–28)

To God belongs
Whatever is in the heavens,
And on earth,
And to Him,
Is the religion, always. *

Invite all to the way of your Lord
With wisdom and beautiful preaching,
And dispute with them in ways
That are best and most gracious. **

---

*   (16: 52)
**   (16: 125)

Call upon Allah,
Or call upon the All-Merciful.
By whatever name you call upon Him,
It is well—
For to Him belong
The All-Beautiful Names. *

The things that endure—
Good deeds—
Are best in the sight of your Lord as rewards,
And best as the foundation for hopes. **

Your God is one God.
Whoever expects to meet his Lord,
Let him work righteousness—
And, in the worship of his Lord,
Let him admit no one as partner. ***

---

*   (17: 110)
**   (18: 46)
*** (18: 110)

God increases in guidance
Those who seek guidance. *

But the deity of you all
Is the One God.
There is no god but Him.
He encompasses all things
In His knowledge. **

High is He above
What they attribute to Him. ***

---

*   (19: 76)
**   (20: 98)
***   (21: 22)

God is the Ultimate Truth and Ever-Constant.
It is He Who gives life to the dead,
And it is He Who has power
Over all things. *

God most certainly guides
To a straight path
Those who believe with sincerity. **

To Him belongs all
That is in the heavens and on earth:
For verily God
Is free of all wants,
And worthy of all Praise. ***

---

*   (22: 6)
**   (22: 54)
*** (22:64)

G od is the very Truth
That makes all things manifest. *

I t is He to Whom belongs
The dominion of the heavens and the earth:
No son has He begotten,
Nor has He a partner in His dominion.
It is He Who created all things,
And ordered them in due proportions. **

A nd put your trust in Him
Who lives and dies not,
And celebrate His praise. ***

---

*   (24: 25)
** (25: 2)
*** (25:58)

If any is grateful,
Truly his gratitude
Is a gain for his own soul.
But if any is ungrateful,
Truly my Lord
Is free of all needs,
Supreme in Honor! *

And He is God.
There is no god but Him.
To Him be praise,
At the first and at the last.
His is the command,
And to Him shall you all be brought back. **

Remembrance of God
Is the greatest thing in life,
Without doubt. ***

---

*   (27: 40)
**   (28: 70)
***   (29:45)

Patiently persevere,
For verily,
The promise of God is true.
Nor let those shake your firmness
Who have, themselves,
No certainty of faith. *

Whoever submits his whole self to God
And is a doer of good
Has grasped, indeed,
The most trustworthy hand-hold.
And with God rests
The end and decision
Of all affairs. **

---

*   (30: 60)
**   (31: 22)

What God,
Out of His Mercy,
Bestows on mankind,
None can withhold.
What He does withhold,
None can grant apart from Him.
And He is the Exalted in Power,
Full of Wisdom. *

O mankind! Call to mind
The grace of God unto you!
Is there a creator, other than God,
To give you sustenance
From heaven or earth?
There is no god but Him.
How, then, are you deluded away from the Truth? **

_____

*   (35: 2)
**   (35: 3)

To God belong
All glory and power;
To Him mount up
All words of purity.
It is He Who
Exalts each deed of righteousness.*

Whoever purifies himself
Does so for the benefit
Of his own soul—
And the destination of all
Is to God. **

---

*   (35: 10)
**   (35: 18)

Verily God knows
All the hidden things
Of the heavens and the earth,
And verily, He has
Full knowledge of all
That is in everyone's hearts. *

This is only a Reminder
For all conscious beings.
And you will certainly know the truth
Of it all after a while. **

God is the Creator of all things,
And He is the Guardian
And Disposer of all affairs. ***

*   (35: 38)
**   (38: 87-88)
*** (39: 62)

He is the Living One.
There is no god but Him.
So pray unto Him,
Making religion pure, for Him only.
Praise be to God,
The Lord of the worlds!*

There is nothing whatever like Him,
And He is the One Who sees
And hears all things. **

Verily,
In the heavens and the earth
Are signs for those who believe. ***

———————————————

*   (40: 65)
**   (42: 11)
***   (45: 3)

T ell those who believe
To forgive
Those who do not look forward
To the Days of God.
It is for Him to recompense
For good or ill, all people,
According to what they have earned. *

G od created the heavens and the earth
For just ends,
And in order that each soul
May find the recompense
Of what it has earned,
And none of them will be wronged.**

G od is free of all wants—
It is you who are needy.***

---

*   (45: 14)
**   (45: 22)
***   (47: 38)

G od loves those Who are fair and just. *

V erily the most honored of you
In the sight of God
Is he who is the most righteous of you.
And God has full knowledge,
And is well acquainted with all things.**

V erily, God knows the secrets
Of the heavens and the earth,
And God sees well
All that you do.***

_____

*   (49: 9)
**   (49: 13)
***   (49: 18)

On the earth are signs for those of assured faith,
as also in your own selves—Will you not then see? *

For God is He Who gives all sustenance—
Lord of all might, Steadfast forever. **

*   (51: 20-21)
** (51: 58)

He is the First
And the Last,
The Evident
And the Immanent. *

He knows what enters
Within the earth
And what comes forth out of it—
What comes down from heaven,
And what mounts up to it.
And He is with you wherever you may be.
And God sees well
All that you do.**

---

*   (57: 3)
**   (57: 4)

Has not the time arrived
For the believers,
That their hearts, in all humility,
Should engage in the remembrance of God
And of the truth
Which has been revealed to them,
And that they should not become
Like those to whom was given Revelation before,
But long ages passed over them
And their hearts grew hard? *

Those saved from the covetousness
Of their own souls—
They are the ones
Who achieve prosperity. **

---

*   (57: 16)
**   (59: 9)

God is He
Other than Whom there is no deity;
He Who knows all things, both secret and open;
He Who is the All-Merciful, the All-Compassionate.
God is He,
Other than Whom there is no deity—
The Sovereign, the Holy One,
The Source of Peace and Perfection,
The Guardian of Faith, the Preserver of Safety,
The Exalted in Might, the Irresistible, and the Supreme!
Glory to God! High is He
Above the partners they attribute to Him!
He is God, the Creator, the All-Holy Maker,
And the All-Fashioning.
To Him belong the All-Beautiful Names!
Whatever is in the heavens and on earth
Declares His Praises and Glory!
He is the Exalted in Might, the All-Wise! *

---

*   (59: 22-24)

Whatever is in the heavens
And on earth
Does declare the Praises
And Glory of God—
The Sovereign, the Holy One,
The Exalted in Might, the All-Wise.*

If any one believes in God,
God guides his heart aright—
For God knows all things.**

God—There is no god but He.
And on God, therefore,
Let the believers
Put their trust. ***

-----

*   (62: 1)
**   (64: 11)
*** (64: 13)

S uch is the admonition given to those
  Who believe in God and the Last Day.
  For those who fear and obey God,
  He ever prepares a way out,
  And He provides for them from sources
  They could never imagine.
  And if they put their trust in God,
  Sufficient is God for them.
  For God surely attains His purpose.
  Verily, for all things,
  God has appointed a due proportion. *

T his is nothing less
  Than a Message
  To all the worlds.**

V erily,
It is truth of assured certainty.
So glorify the name of your Lord, Most High. *

A nd whatever good you send forth
For your souls,
You will find it in God's presence—
Even better, and greater, in reward.
So seek the Grace of God,
For God is All-Forgiving, All-Compassionate. **

N one can know the forces
Of your Lord except Him,
And this is nothing other than
A warning for mankind. ***

---

*   (69: 51–52)
**   (73: 20)
*** (74: 31)

Does man think
That he will be left unattended,
Without purpose? *

Has there not been over man
A long period of time,
When he was nothing—
Not even mentioned? **

Then what Message,
After this,
Will they believe in? ***

_____

*   (75: 36)
**   (76: 1)
***   (77: 50)

Therefore, whoever wills—
Let him take a straight path
To his Lord! *

For it is indeed
A Message of instruction.
Therefore, whoever wills—
Let him keep it in remembrance.**

Verily,
This is no less than a Message
To all the worlds,
With benefits to whomever among you
Wills to go straight. ***

---

*   (78: 39)
**   (80: 11—12)
***   (81: 27—28)